open-top bus for sightseeing

motorbike

bicycle

mouse racing car in the lead

Published in the USA by
Rand McNally & Company
Copyright © 1977 Purnell & Sons Limited
Printed in Italy
ISBN 0-528-82040-0
Library of Congress Catalog Card Number 77-2601

Things That Go
WORD BOOK

Illustrated by
Hutchings

Rand McNally & Company

CHICAGO / NEW YORK / SAN FRANCISCO

Automobile

oars

trunk lid

boat

trunk

seat springs

axle

bumper

hub-cap

tire

crab apple

Hydrofoil

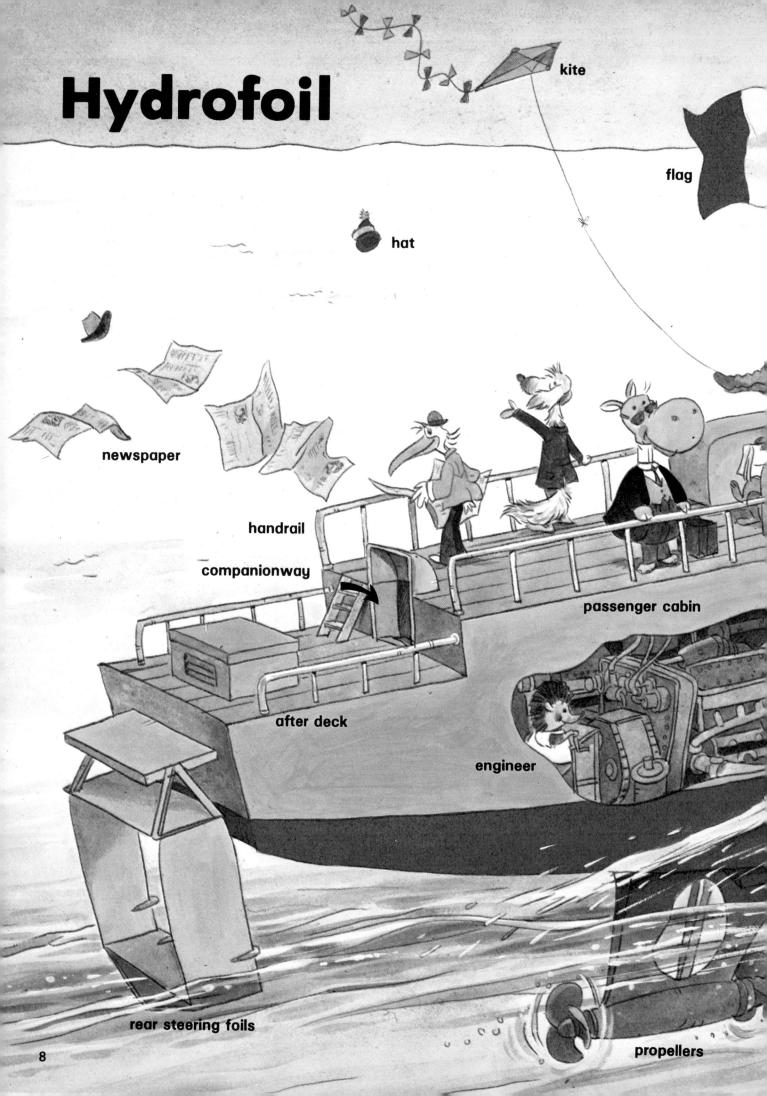

kite

flag

hat

newspaper

handrail

companionway

passenger cabin

after deck

engineer

rear steering foils

propellers

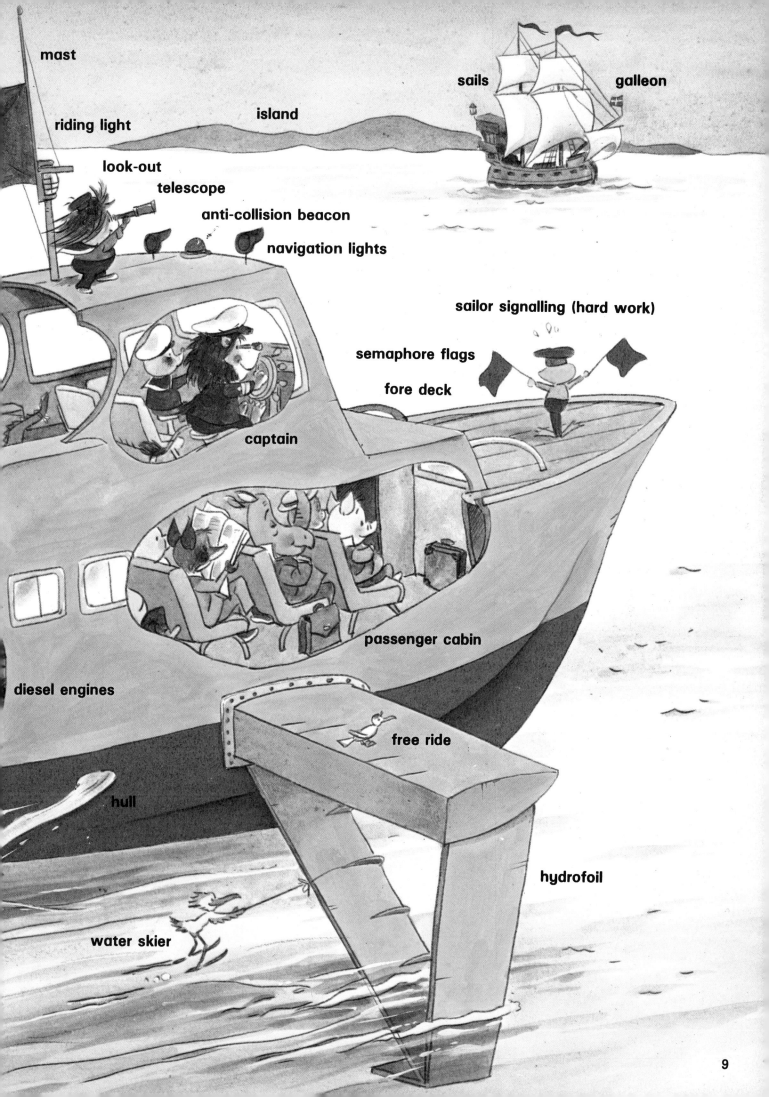

mast

riding light

look-out

telescope

anti-collision beacon

navigation lights

island

sails

galleon

sailor signalling (hard work)

semaphore flags

fore deck

captain

passenger cabin

diesel engines

free ride

hull

hydrofoil

water skier

Earth Movers

jib

excavator

gear wheels

shovel

wheelbarrow

hitch-hiker

irate caterpillar

tool box

Caterpillar track

blade

10

double-decker
digger

dumptruck

hydraulic ram

earth leveller

foreman

coffee break

pick

tired

time off

11

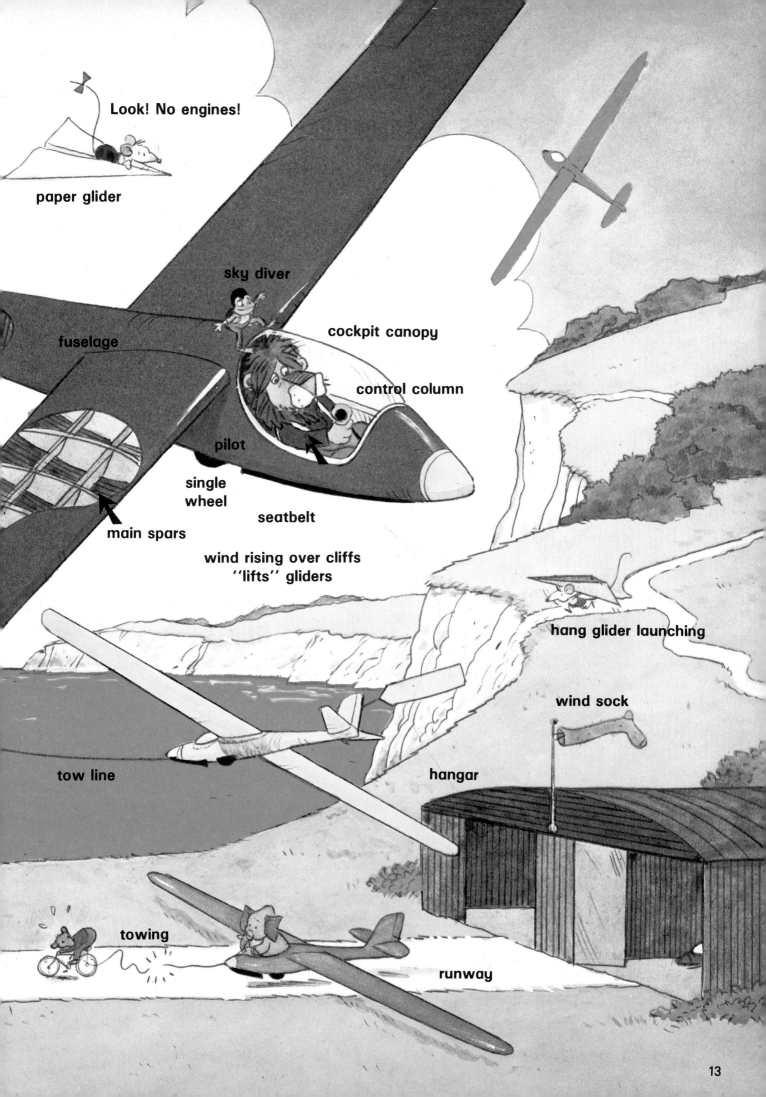

Look! No engines!

paper glider

sky diver

cockpit canopy

fuselage

control column

pilot

single wheel

seatbelt

main spars

wind rising over cliffs "lifts" gliders

hang glider launching

wind sock

tow line

hangar

towing

runway

13

Traction Engine

high jump

canopy

flywheel

coal bunker

driving gears

oil lamp

hub

help

audience

floodlight

oops!

14

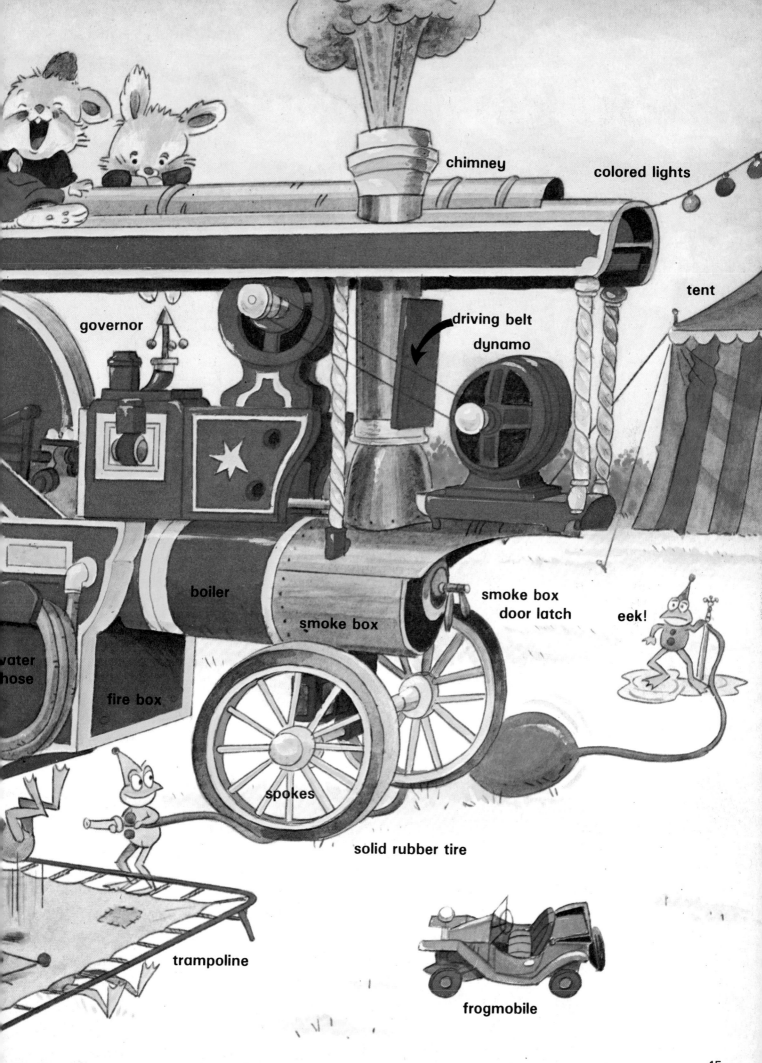

chimney

colored lights

tent

driving belt

dynamo

governor

boiler

smoke box

smoke box door latch

eek!

water hose

fire box

spokes

solid rubber tire

trampoline

frogmobile

15

Hovercraft

propeller

disembarkation
ramp

engine

engine air intake

skirt

ticket office

waiting cars

16

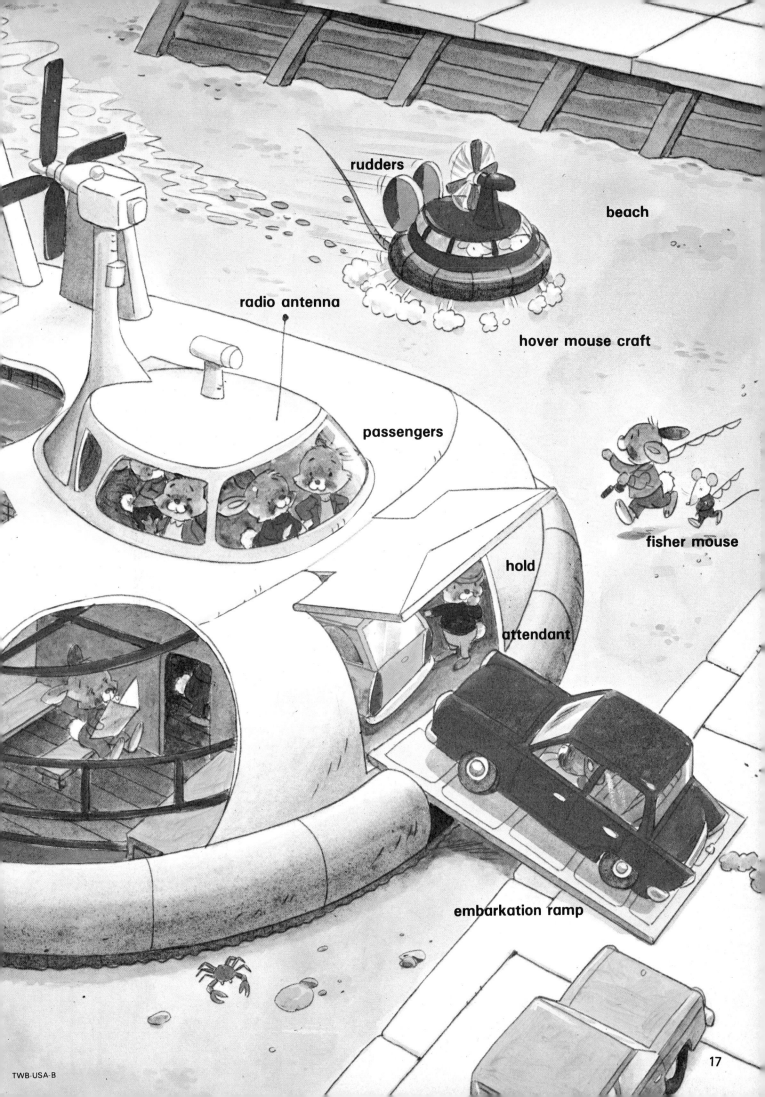

rudders

beach

radio antenna

hover mouse craft

passengers

fisher mouse

hold

attendant

embarkation ramp

Bus

kite

open top deck

passengers

old-fashioned bus

driver

hiss!

oil lamp

radiator

outside gear levers

solid rubber tire

spoked wheel

pedestrians

18

outside staircase

turn signal

windshield

head lights

double-decker bus

lost luggage

pavement

mouse airport bus

road

19

Under the sea

captain

smoke stack

stowaway

chock　lifeboat

portholes

school of fish

rudder

propeller

diver

bathyscaphe

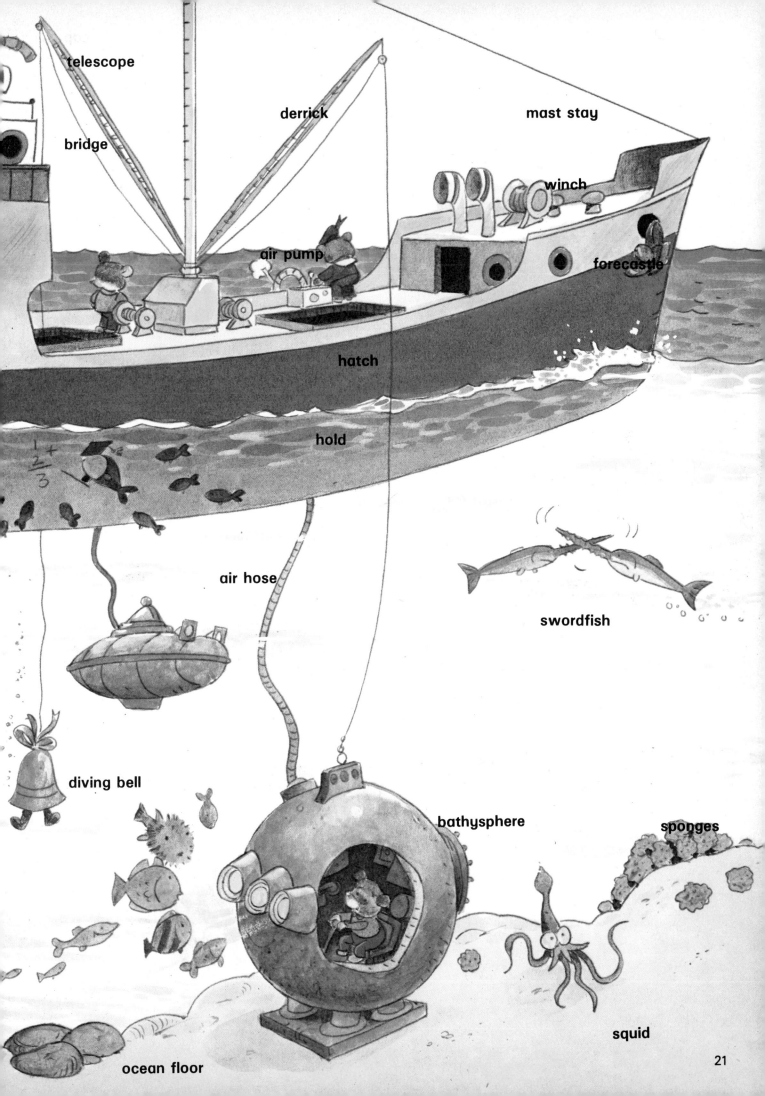

telescope

derrick

mast stay

bridge

winch

air pump

forecastle

hatch

hold

air hose

swordfish

diving bell

bathysphere

sponges

ocean floor

squid

21

Jumbo Boeing 747

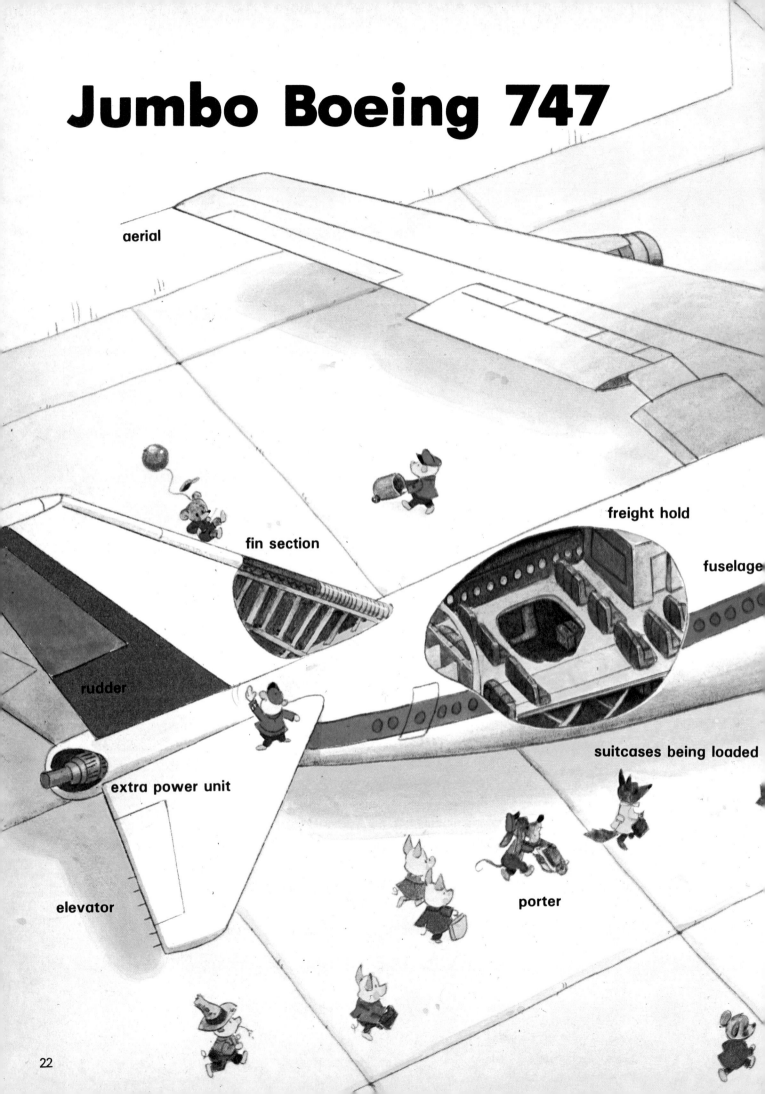

aerial

fin section

freight hold

fuselage

rudder

extra power unit

suitcases being loaded

elevator

porter

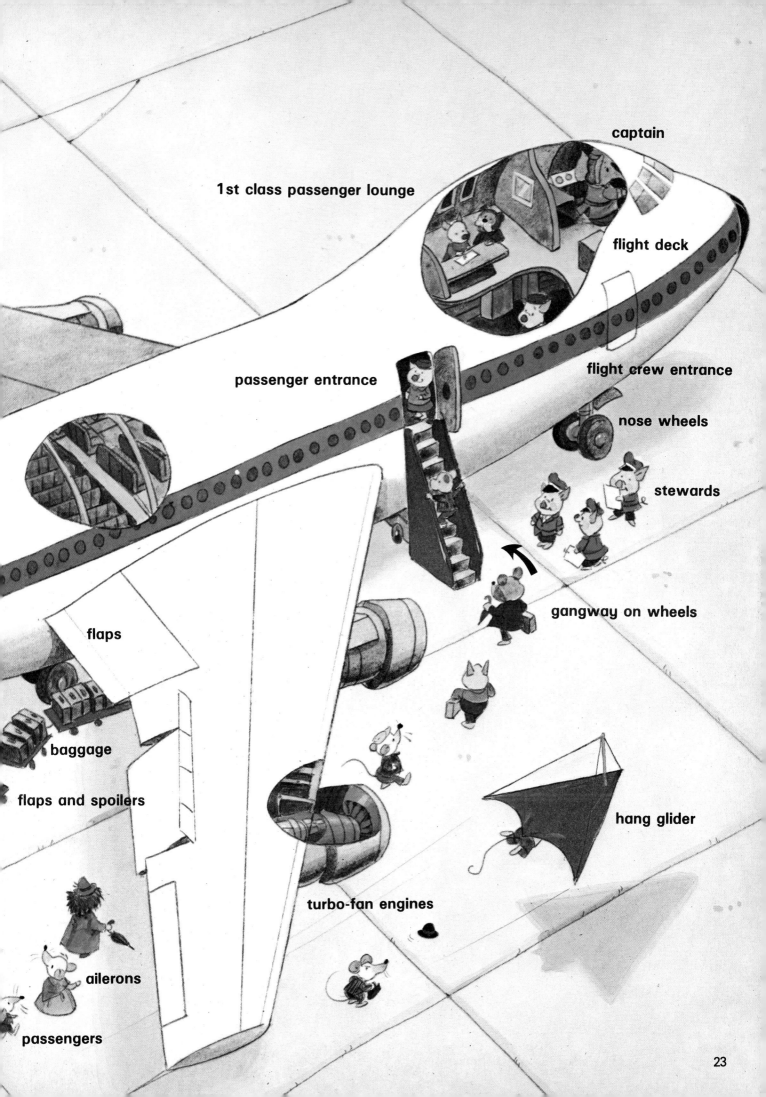

captain

1st class passenger lounge

flight deck

passenger entrance

flight crew entrance

nose wheels

stewards

gangway on wheels

flaps

baggage

flaps and spoilers

hang glider

turbo-fan engines

ailerons

passengers

23

Cement Mixer

peeping tom

steering lever

bulldozer

fuel tank

hydraulic cylinders

hod

blade

Caterpillar tracks

runaway wheelbarrow

water stand-pipe

hose

shovel

wet cement

float

wooden shuttering

Traffic

NEWSSTAND

very old taxi

traffic jam

filling up with gas (and air!)

motor scooter

airhose

cheese buggy

27

Helicopter

cloud

tail rotor blades

fuselage formers

bug copter

transport helicopter

crop duster

tank

major calamity

28

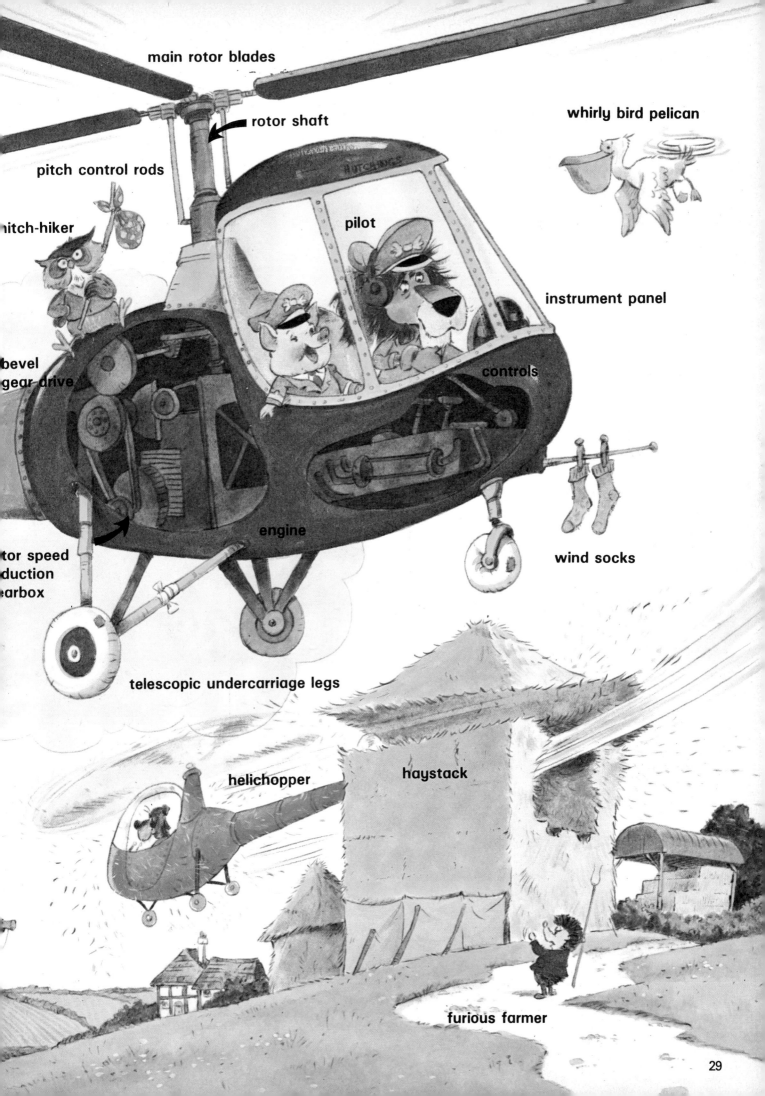

main rotor blades

rotor shaft

whirly bird pelican

pitch control rods

hitch-hiker

pilot

instrument panel

bevel gear-drive

controls

rotor speed reduction gearbox

engine

wind socks

telescopic undercarriage legs

helichopper

haystack

furious farmer

Cabin Cruiser

fisherpig

navigation lights

foghorn

flag

skipper

helmsman

wheel

throttle
(go faster)

wheelhouse

stern

engine

piston

steering gear

propeller shaft

crankshaft

exhaust and engine
cooling water

forward/reverse gear box

rudder

propeller

marker buoy

water skier

sun bather

mast

anchor

handrail

hatch

deck

belt

cook

cabin

net

fed-up frog

sunny side up!

frames

obstacle (flotsam or jetsam)

snorkel

twin-hulled catamaran

speedboat

reeds

31

Combine Harvester

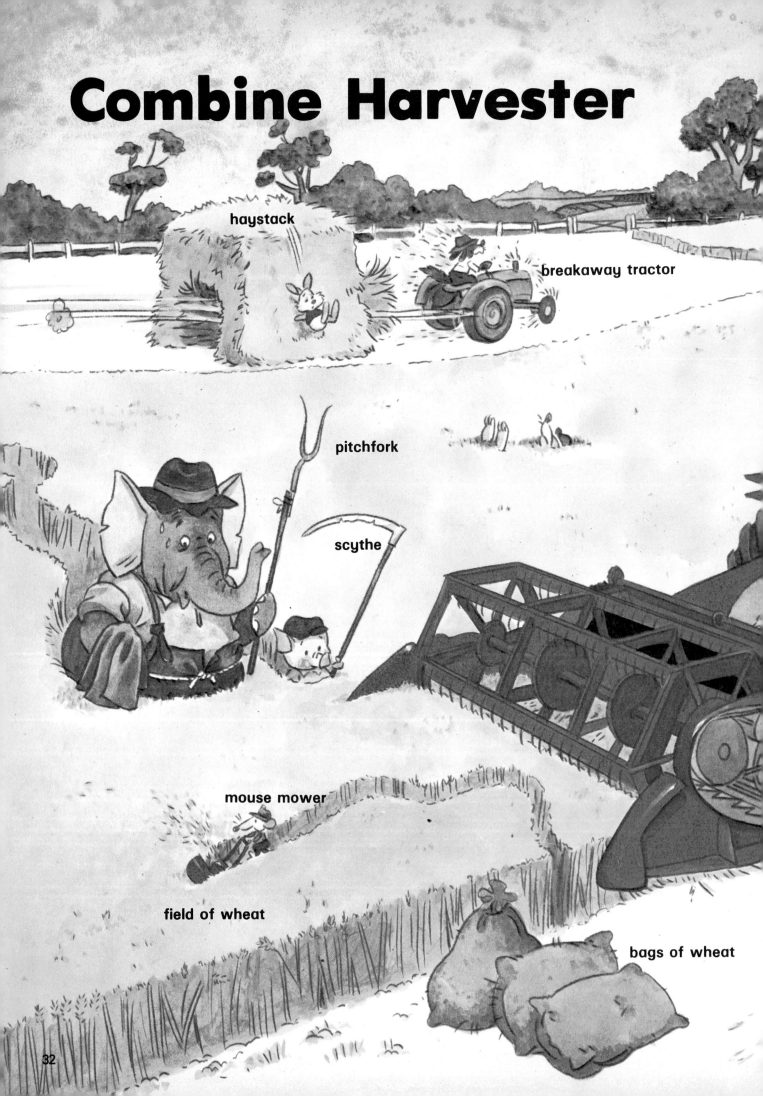

haystack

breakaway tractor

pitchfork

scythe

mouse mower

field of wheat

bags of wheat

scared crows

dog tired

farmhouse

flutterby

driver

let's have lunch

scarecrow

conveyor belt

steering wheel

grain truck

ouch!

rake

ladybug laborer

HUTCHINGS

Bomber and Fighters

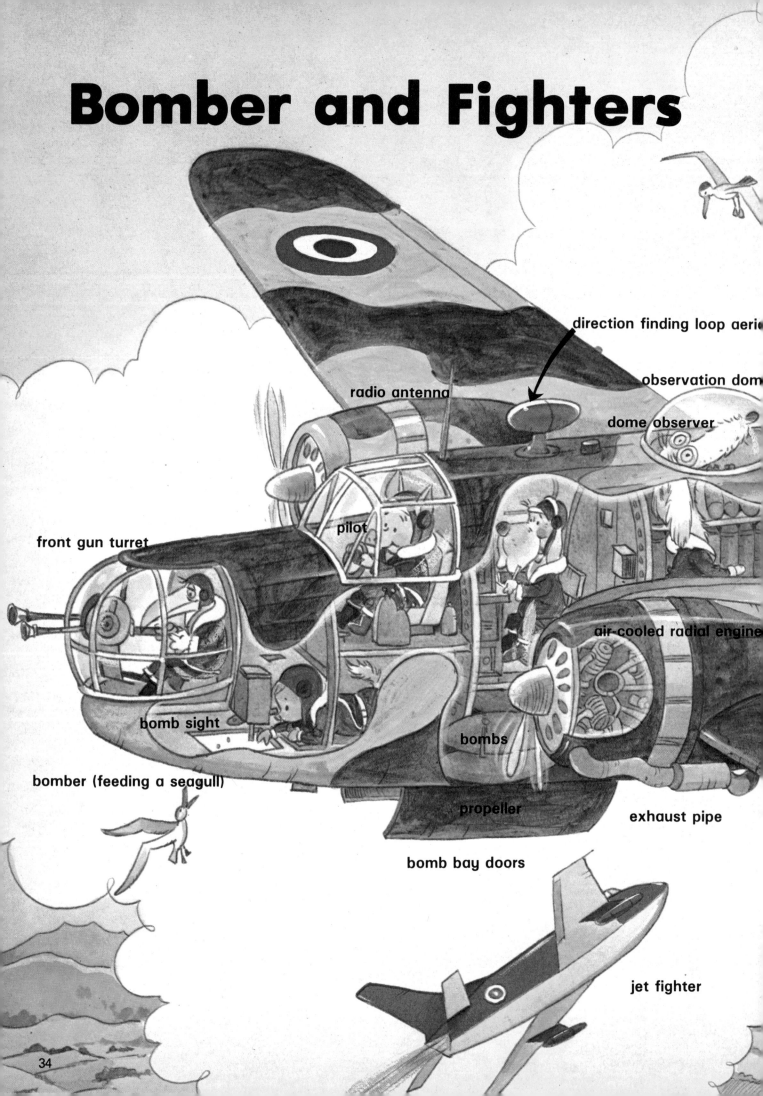

direction finding loop aeria

observation dom

dome observer

radio antenna

front gun turret

pilot

air-cooled radial engine

bomb sight

bombs

bomber (feeding a seagull)

propeller

exhaust pipe

bomb bay doors

jet fighter

34

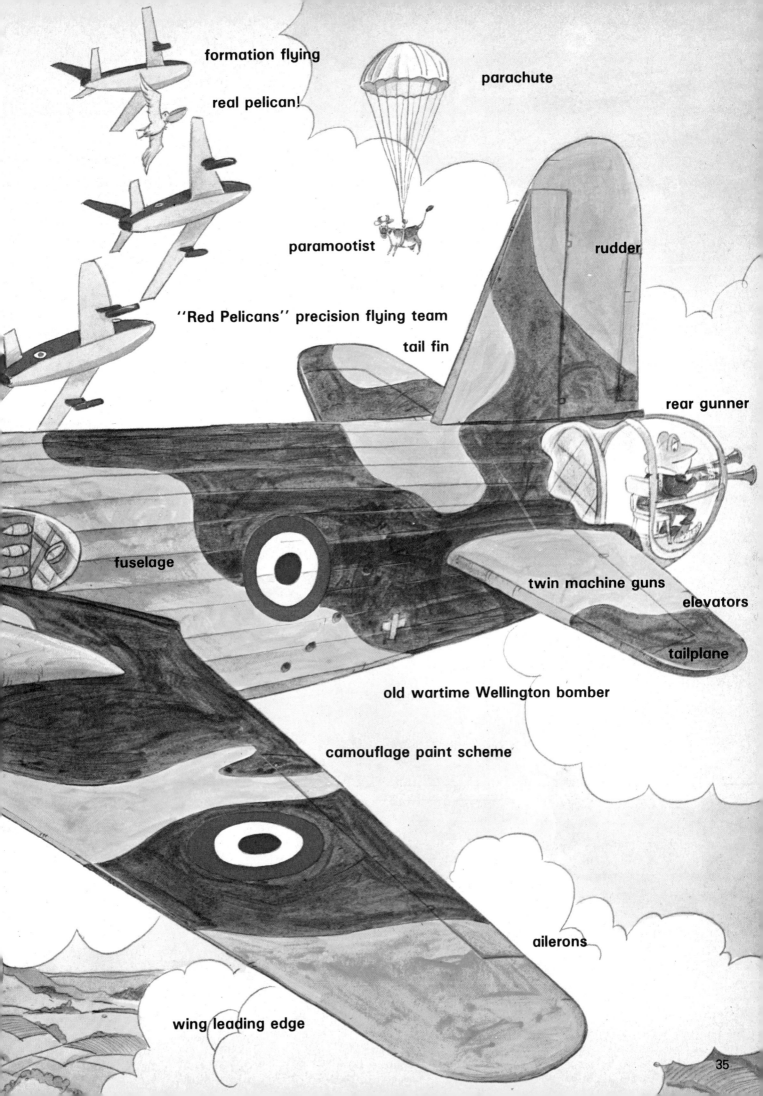

Stock Car

straw bales

exhaust pipe

race track

tire marks

flying fox

competitor's number

chopper seat

collision

up and over doo

safety barrier

competitor from another race

back seat driver

pity! mouse is in the wrong race!

fearless driver

bump!

windshield

flying spring

flat tire

spare wheel

protected headlight glass

bumper

Car Ferry

mast

ship's flag

stowaway

wheel

docking bridge

containers

ramp closes to form watertight door

rudders

propeller

car

carp

smoke

captain

smokestack

searchlight

ventilators

davits

bridge

lifeboat

able alligator

portholes

bunks

cabins

vehicle deck

hull

engines

boiler room

waterline

dinghy

39

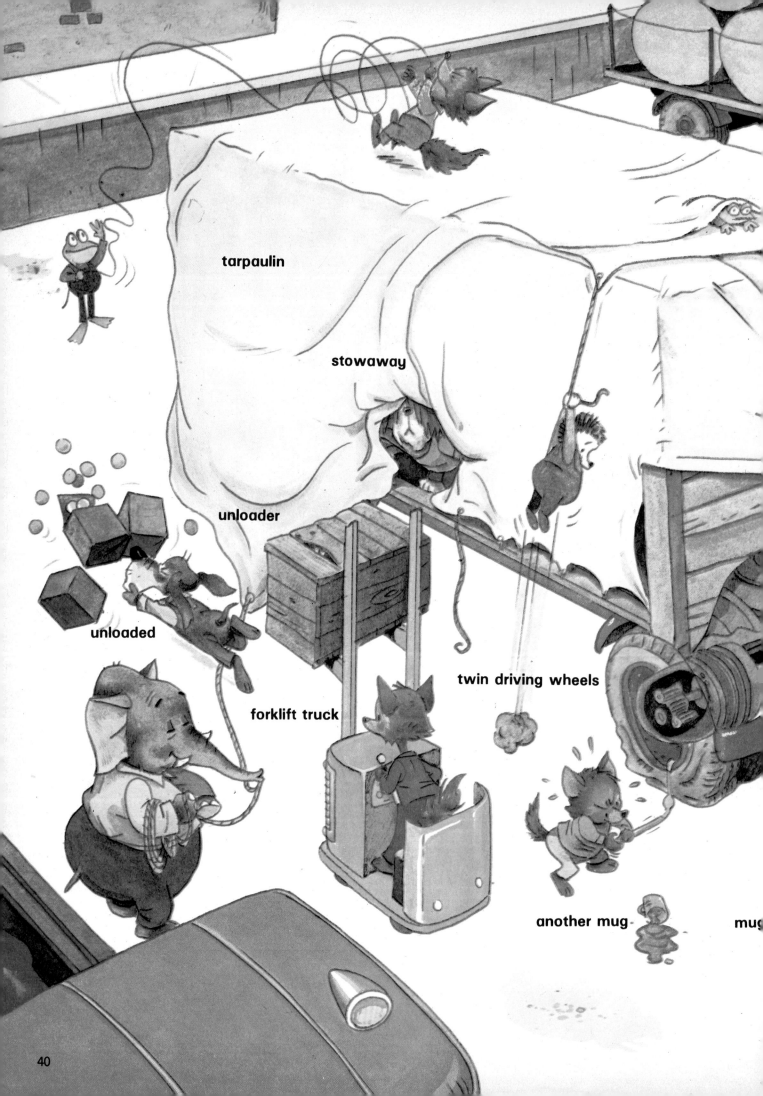

tarpaulin

stowaway

unloader

unloaded

forklift truck

twin driving wheels

another mug

mug

Semitrailer

trailer

cab

diesel engine

driving axle

filler cap

fuel tank

gearbox

engine cooling fan

tool box

truck driver

Concorde

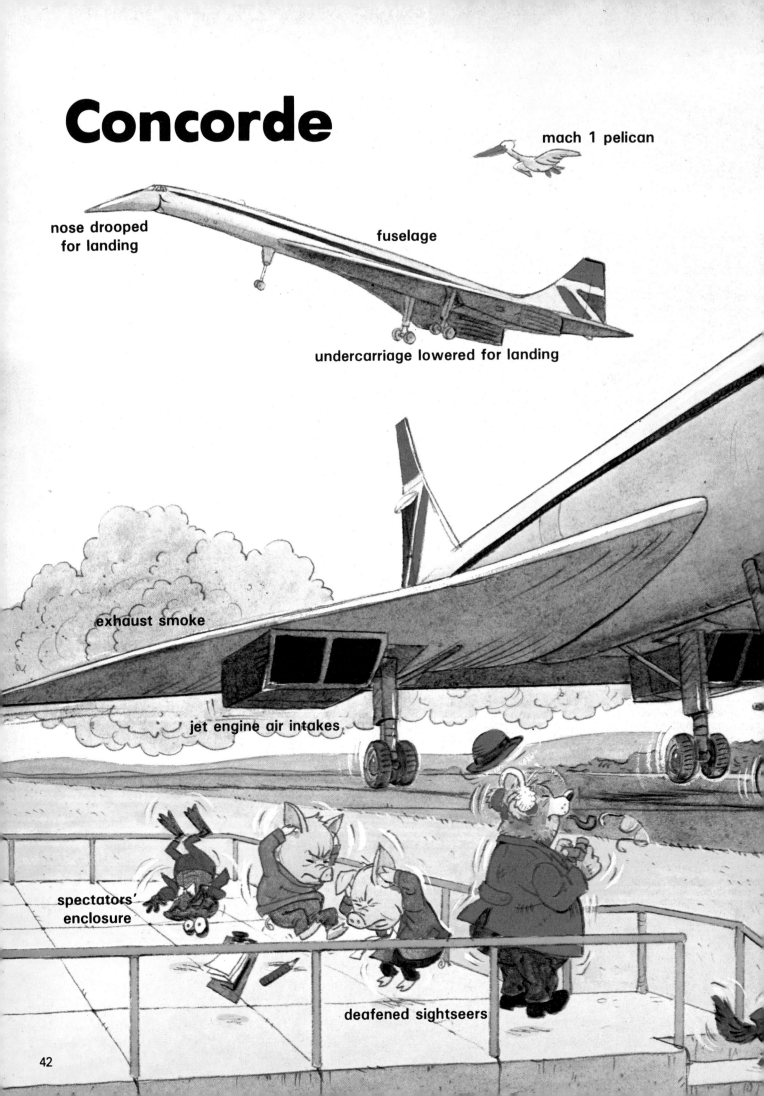

mach 1 pelican

nose drooped
for landing

fuselage

undercarriage lowered for landing

exhaust smoke

jet engine air intakes

spectators'
enclosure

deafened sightseers

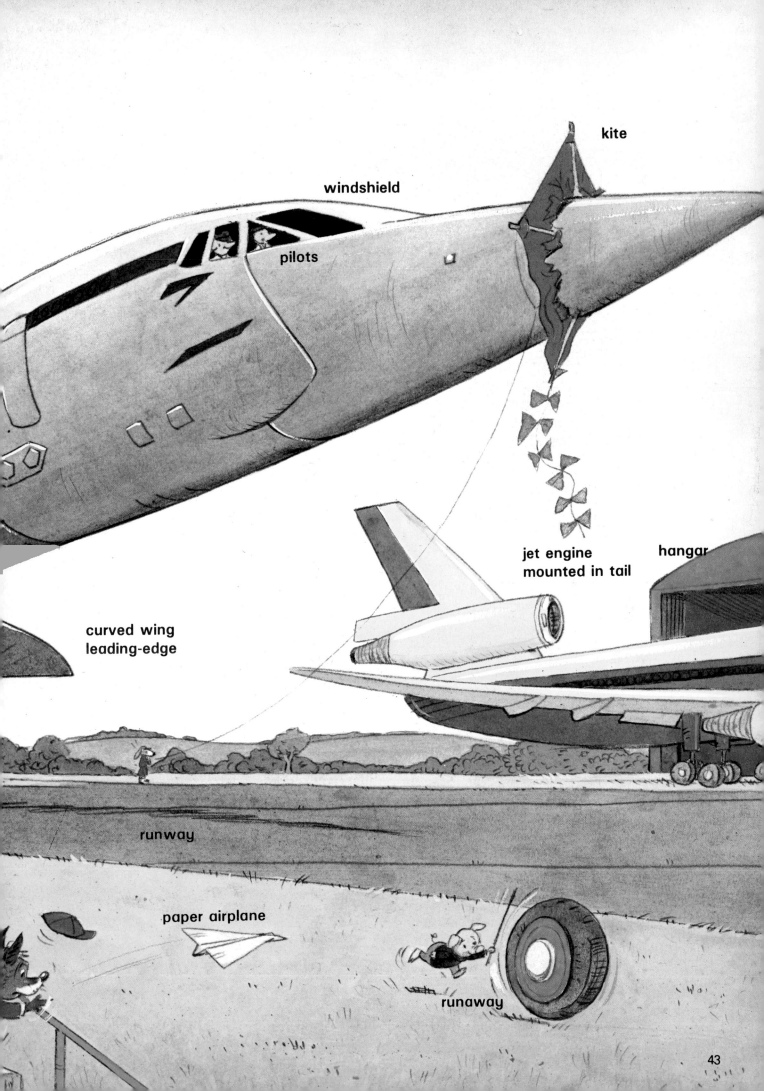

kite

windshield

pilots

jet engine
mounted in tail

hangar

curved wing
leading-edge

runway

paper airplane

runaway

43

Tank

washing

gun turret

radio antenna

heavy tank

cap

your turn nex

bonnet

medium tank

baby tank

fish tank

snail shell

tank tracks

44

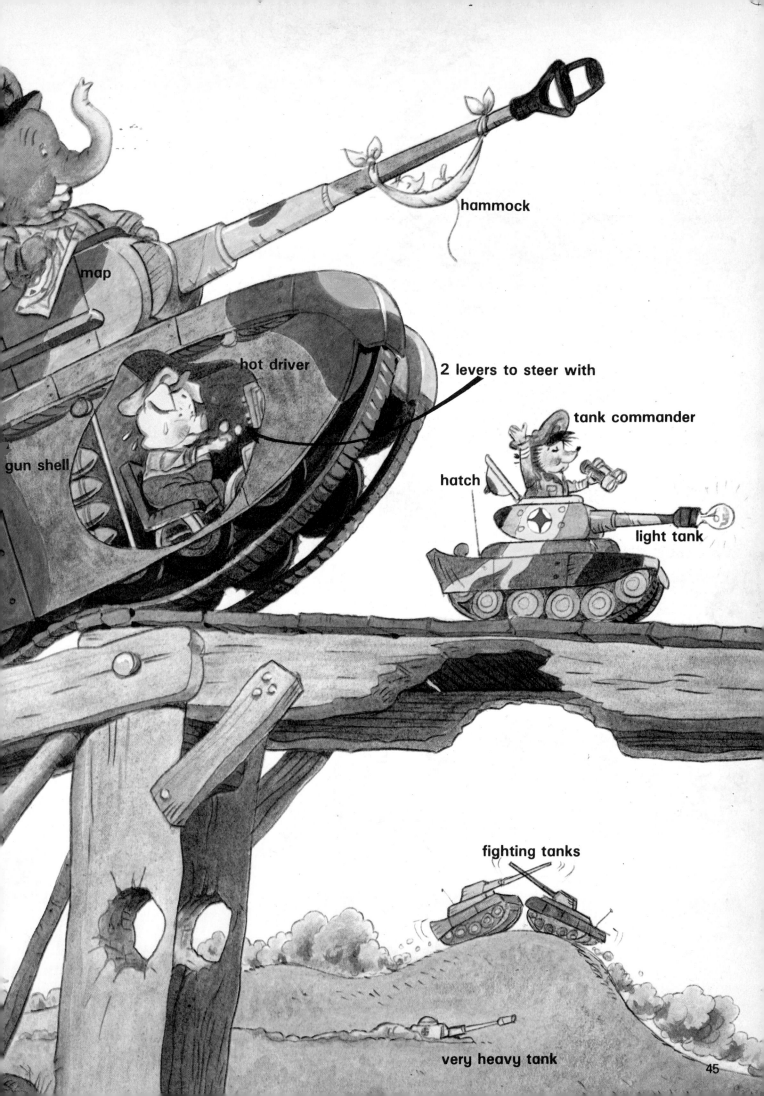

Racing Car

safety barrier

engine air intake

roll bar

radiator
air intake

HUTCHINGS

10

airfool?

airfoil

very wide racing tires

official starter

checkered flag

7

road runner?

46

spectators

crash helmet

goggles

front suspension

Stirling Mouse

47

Aircraft carrier

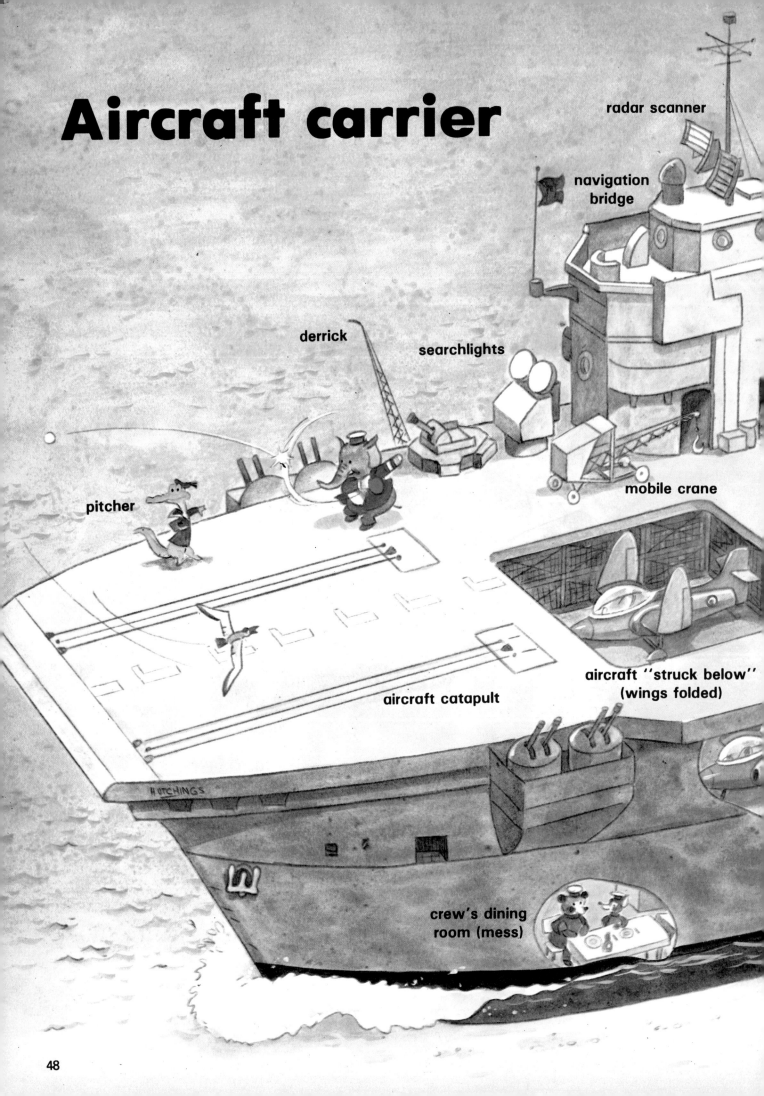

radar scanner

navigation bridge

derrick

searchlights

mobile crane

pitcher

aircraft "struck below" (wings folded)

aircraft catapult

crew's dining room (mess)

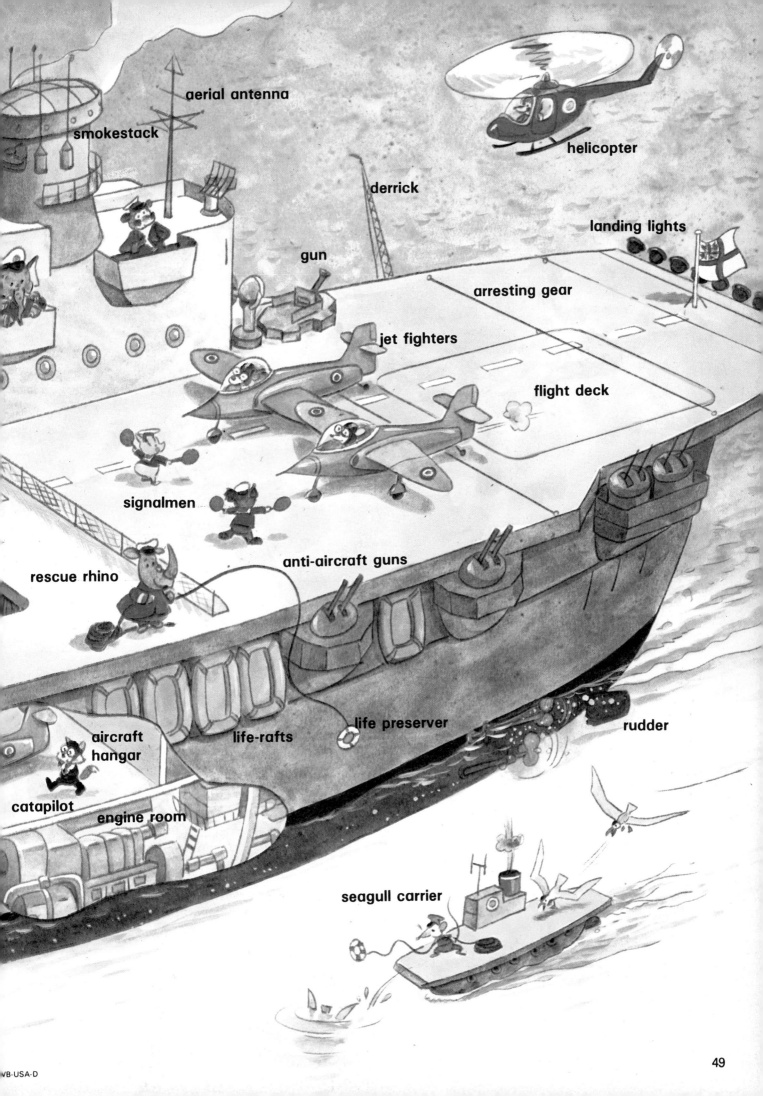

aerial antenna

smokestack

helicopter

derrick

landing lights

gun

arresting gear

jet fighters

flight deck

signalmen

anti-aircraft guns

rescue rhino

life preserver

rudder

aircraft hangar

life-rafts

catapilot

engine room

seagull carrier

Cargo Plane

light aircraft

propellers

captain

co-pilot

radial engines

flight deck

navigator

cargo decks

hold

nose wheels

main wheels

jumbo air ferry

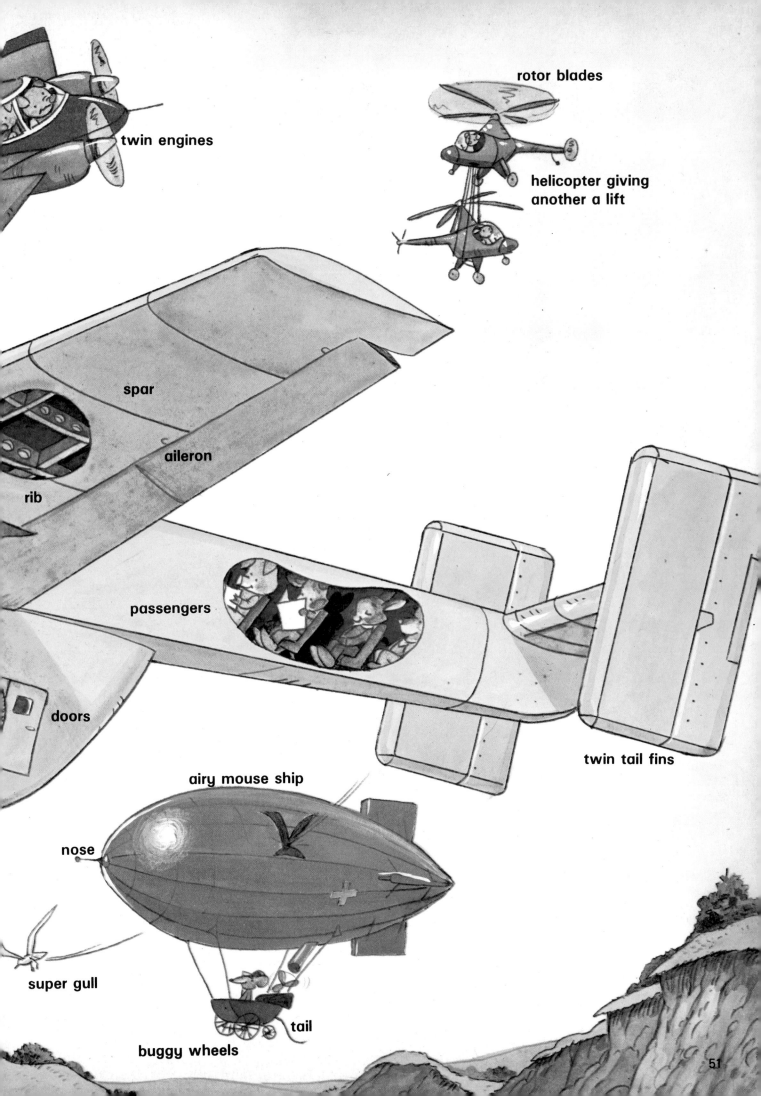

twin engines

rotor blades

helicopter giving
another a lift

spar

aileron

rib

passengers

doors

twin tail fins

airy mouse ship

nose

super gull

tail

buggy wheels

51

Submarine

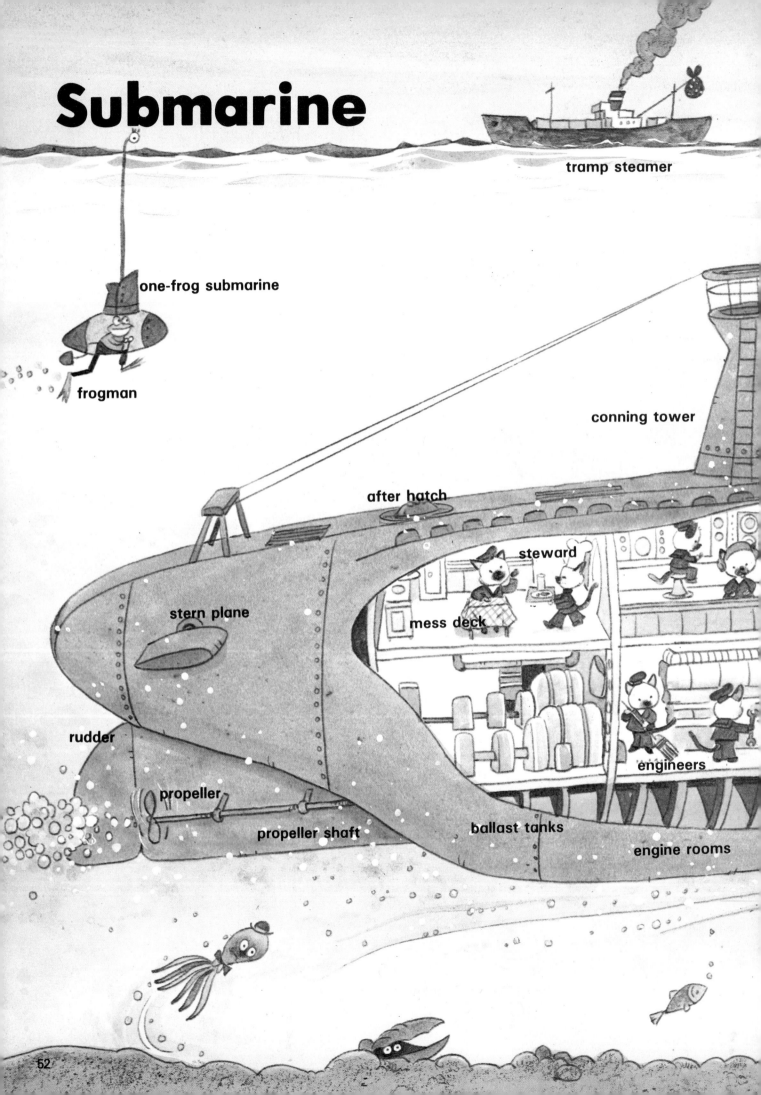

tramp steamer

one-frog submarine

frogman

conning tower

after hatch

steward

stern plane

mess deck

engineers

rudder

propeller

propeller shaft

ballast tanks

engine rooms

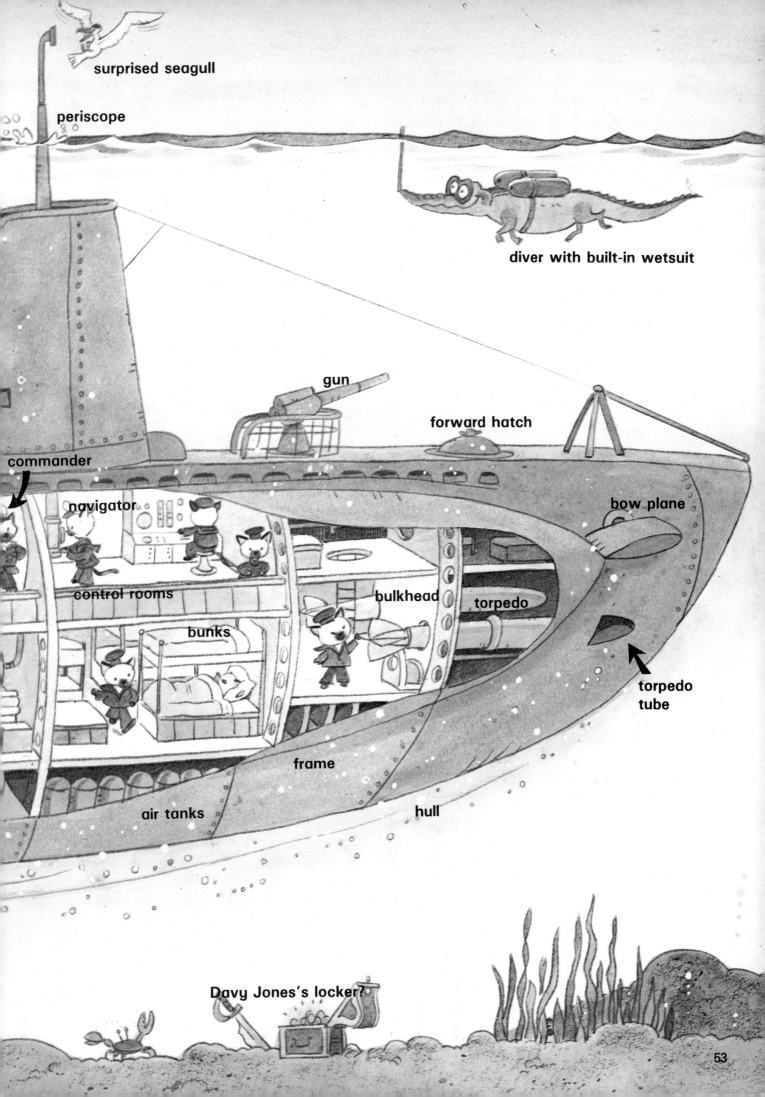

surprised seagull

periscope

diver with built-in wetsuit

gun

forward hatch

commander

navigator

bow plane

control rooms

bulkhead

torpedo

bunks

torpedo tube

frame

air tanks

hull

Davy Jones's locker?

Locomotive

water tower

freight car

coal

fireman

driver

driving wheels

railroad tie

toad being towed

luggage

luggage cart

porter

incubator
baby buggy

Space-laboratory

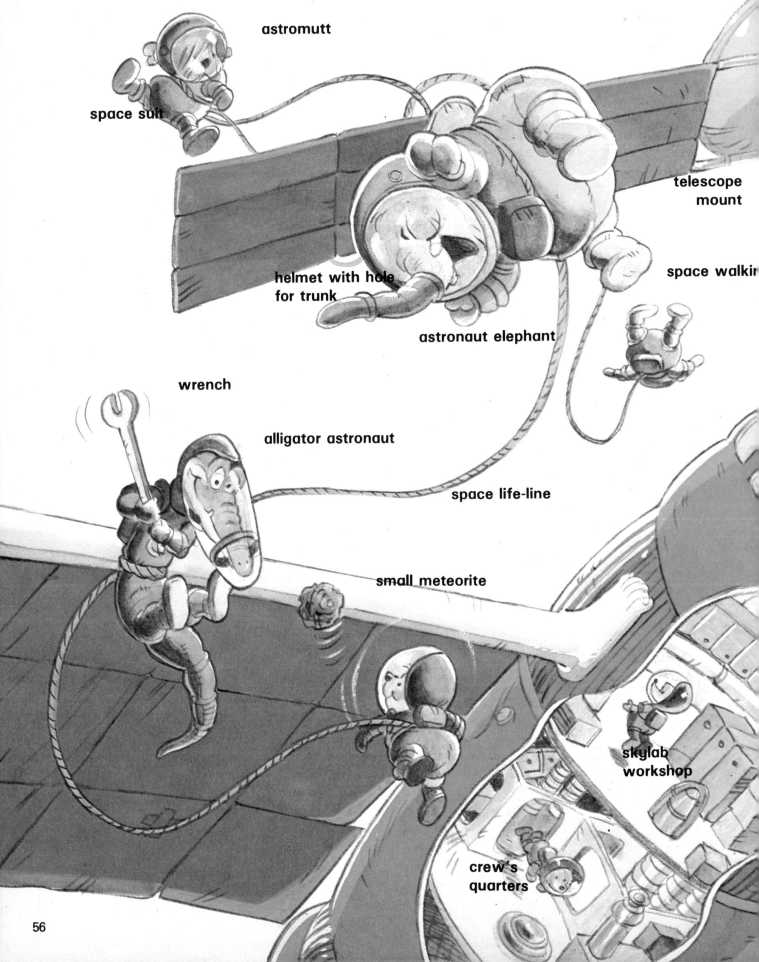

astromutt

space suit

telescope mount

helmet with hole for trunk

space walkin

astronaut elephant

wrench

alligator astronaut

space life-line

small meteorite

skylab workshop

crew's quarters

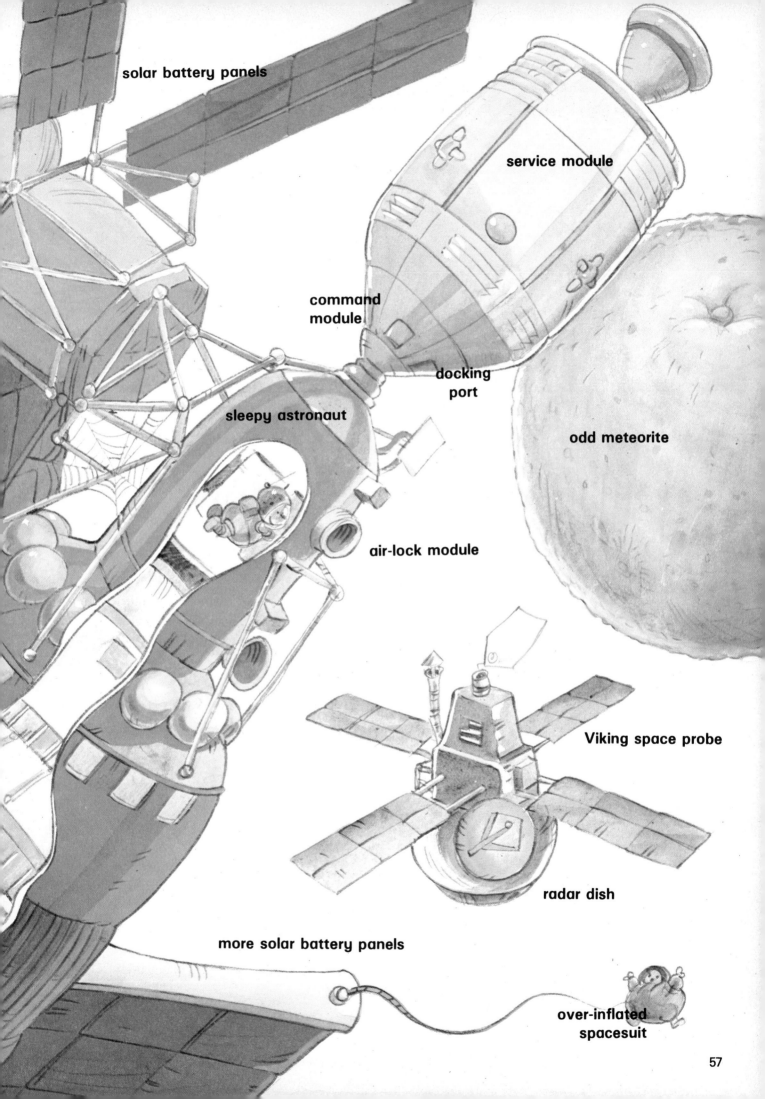

solar battery panels

service module

command
module

docking
port

sleepy astronaut

odd meteorite

air-lock module

Viking space probe

radar dish

more solar battery panels

over-inflated
spacesuit

57

Dredger

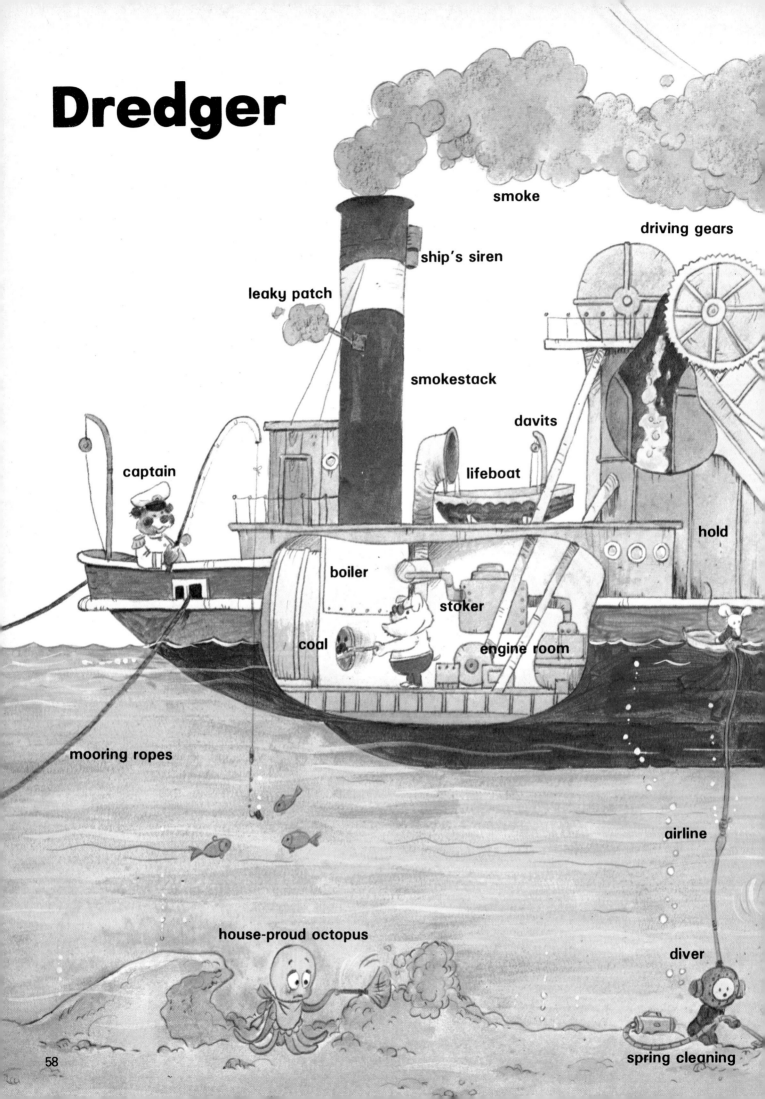

smoke

driving gears

ship's siren

leaky patch

smokestack

davits

lifeboat

captain

hold

boiler

stoker

coal

engine room

mooring ropes

airline

house-proud octopus

diver

spring cleaning

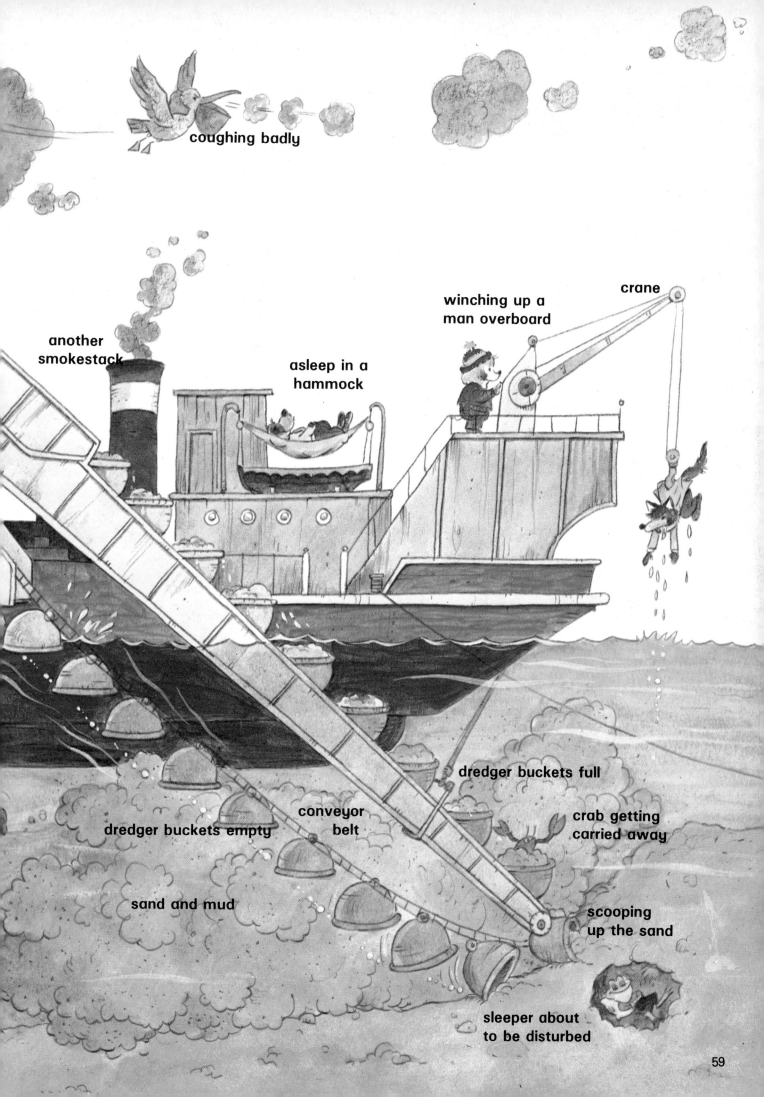

coughing badly

another smokestack

asleep in a hammock

winching up a man overboard

crane

dredger buckets full

conveyor belt

dredger buckets empty

crab getting carried away

sand and mud

scooping up the sand

sleeper about to be disturbed

Fire engine

pelican water service

searchlight

driving mirror

ladder

fire engine engine

hose

accelerator (go faster)

fireman

control valve

mouse to the rescue

fire station

bell

the pole

helmet

fireman in
distress

water-tank

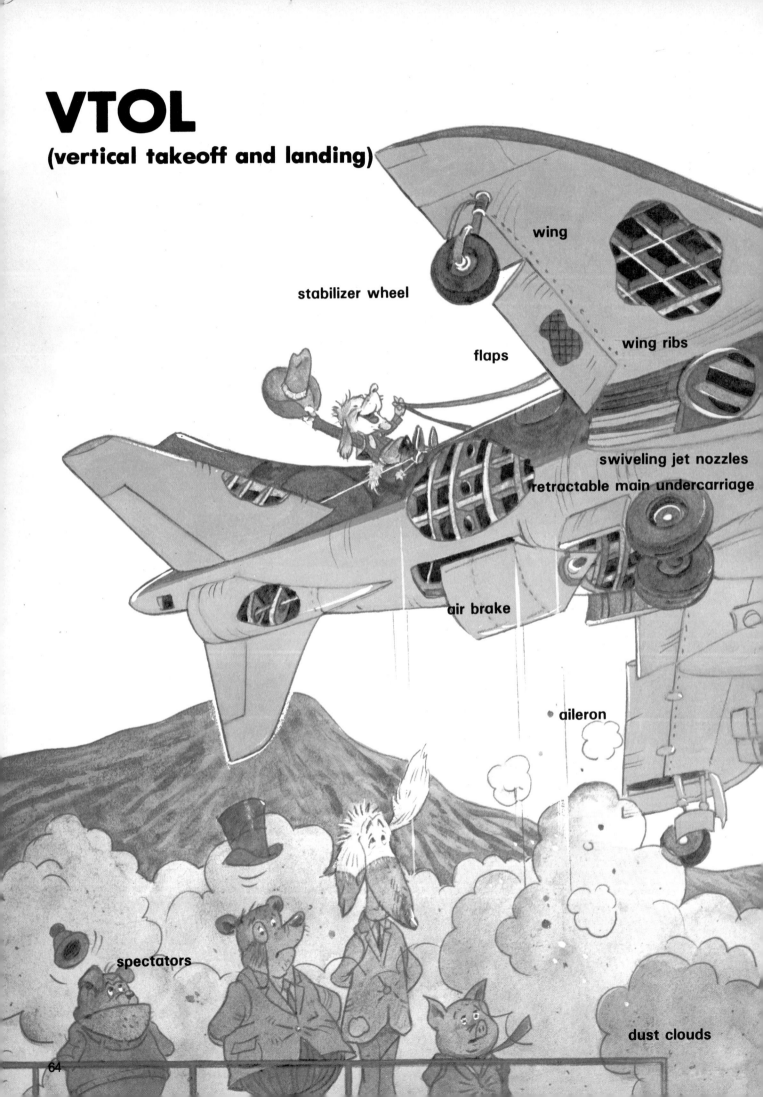

VTOL
(vertical takeoff and landing)

wing

stabilizer wheel

wing ribs

flaps

swiveling jet nozzles

retractable main undercarriage

air brake

aileron

spectators

dust clouds

64

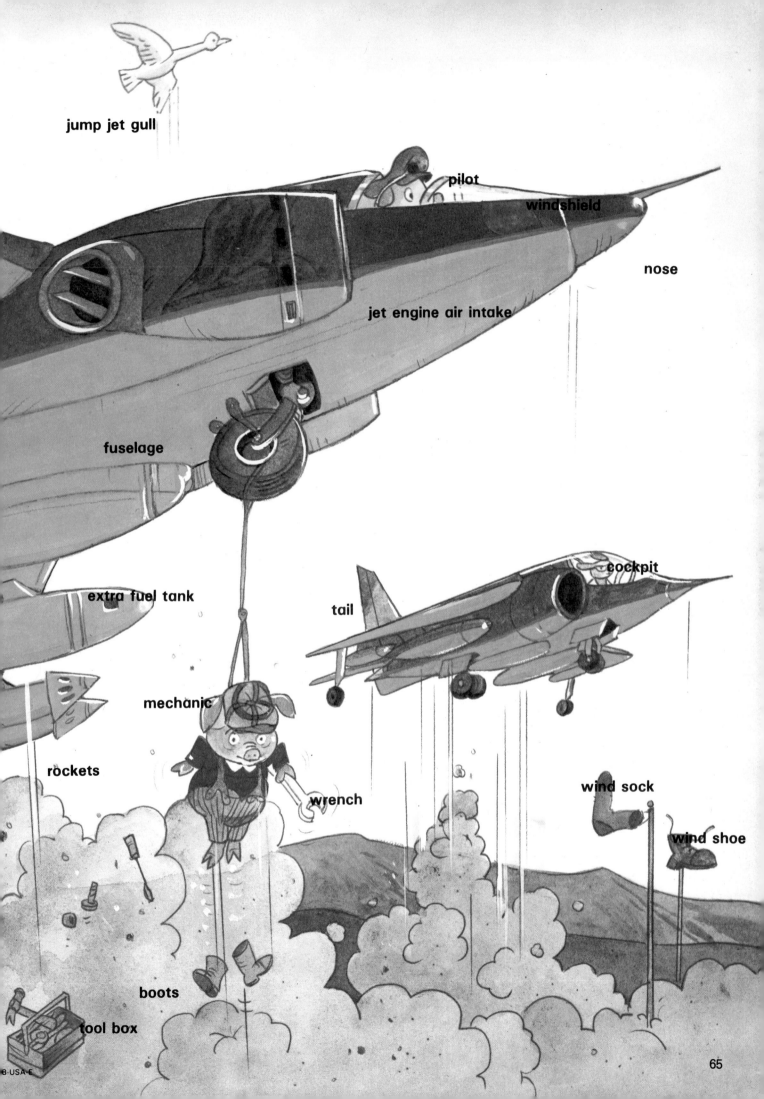

jump jet gull

pilot

windshield

nose

jet engine air intake

fuselage

extra fuel tank

cockpit

tail

mechanic

rockets

wrench

wind sock

wind shoe

boots

tool box

Tractor

haystack

snorkeling

water spraying

mirror

exhaust pipe

hood

fender

radiator grille

engine

gearbox

axle

tire

heave!

digger mouse

leaving home

farmhouse

hang gliding

potato planting

pulling out a tree stump

pick axe

farm hand

plowing

over-eating

67

Liner

flags

kite

smokestacks

captain

deck

lifeboat

rich passengers

davits

sunbathing

stern

stowaway

cook

engine room

galley

water line

dining hall

propeller

cap

stabilizer fin

rowing boat

radar
scanner

albatross

ocean

bridge

splash!

swimming pool

jolly sailor

steward

whoops!

bow

anchor

painting ship

port holes

hold

car going nowhere

cargo

school of fish

On the moon

solar battery panels

skylab

life-line

moon-tennis

crater

rock-collecting

70

steering jet

lunar module

HUTCHINGS

moon-castles

planting a flag

71

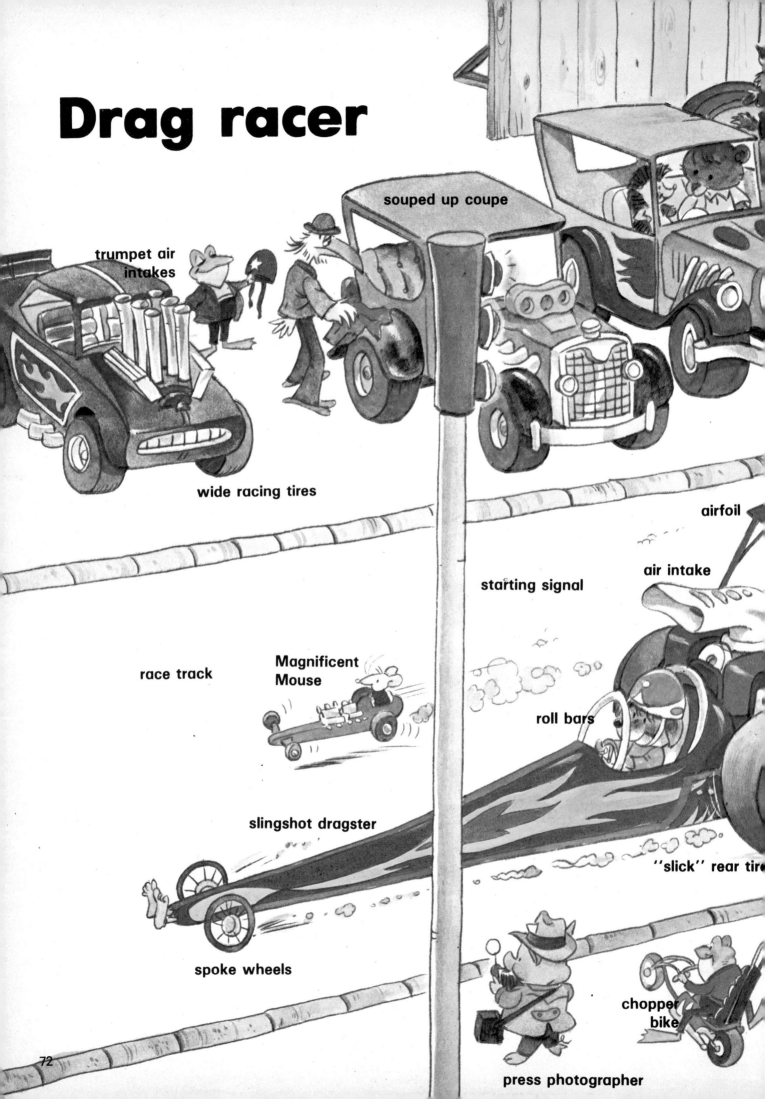

Drag racer

trumpet air
intakes

souped up coupe

wide racing tires

airfoil

air intake

starting signal

race track

Magnificent
Mouse

roll bars

slingshot dragster

"slick" rear tire

spoke wheels

chopper
bike

press photographer

72

Warship

radar mast

flag pole

missile launcher

helicopter

smokestack

flag

safety nets

missiles

lifeboat

rudder

cabin

engine room

boiler room

screws

stabilizers

tender

dock

command car

anti-submarine helicopter

fish dinner

telescope

bridge

gun turrets

anchor (not for fishing)

mess

painting the sailor

sailor painting

hull

bow

soggy froggy

wreck

Biplane

wingtip

spinner

learner driver   (about to stall)

shock absorber

very low flying

water-skiers

air mattress

skin-diver

speedboat

Fearless Fox the wing walker

goggles

flying suit

joystick

rudder pedals

struts

tailwheel

aerobatic pilot (looping the loop)

low flying

very very low flying

wreck

77

bags of garbage

someone
buried in dust

polite frog sweeper

garbage can

untidy cleaner

broom

photographer

tripod

bag with cameras in it